THE EDGE

THE EDGE

POETRY OF LIFE

EDDIE HO

iUniverse, Inc.
Bloomington

THE EDGE
POETRY OF LIFE

iUniverse books may be ordered through booksellers or by contacting:

iUniverse
1663 Liberty Drive
Bloomington, IN 47403
www.iuniverse.com
1-800-Authors (1-800-288-4677)

ISBN: 978-1-4697-3865-9 (sc)
ISBN: 978-1-4697-3866-6 (ebk)

Printed in the United States of America

iUniverse rev. date: 01/30/2012

CONTENTS

PART I: THE SCHOOL DAYS 1

   1. THE SPARTAN OATH 3
   2. TAILSPIN...4
   3. A STUDENT'S PLEA...5
   4. THE PULSE..6
   5. THE IDENTITY CRISIS..7
   6. THE SMOKING PEERS...8
   7. THE TEST DRIVE..9
   8. I'M LEARNING 11
   9. THE DELIVERY 12
  10. THE REGRETFUL STUDENT 14
  11. THE MARK...15

PART II: THE UNFORTUNATE INCIDENTS...................17

  12. THE DEFECT 19
  13. THE LONELY ROAD..20
  14. THE ORPHAN...21
  15. THE STRAY LIFE 22
  16. THE STICKY SITUATION.....................................24
  17. SPECULATION 25
  18. JUVENILE HALL...26
  19. THE SHELTER 27
  20. THE BLIND EYE..28
  21. THE INNOCENT VICTIMS....................................29

PART III: OCCUPATIONAL STATUS 31
   22. THE COMPANY...33
   23. DR. GRINNY HO...34
   24. THE PASTOR..36
   25. THE TEACHER...38
   26. THE SOCIAL WORKER...39
   27. THE ENTERTAINER...40
   28. THE QUESTION MARK...41
   29. THE COACH..42
   30. THE STATUS SYMBOL..43

PART IV: THE PRICELESS WONDERS 45
   31. A NEW LIFE..47
   32. THE ROMANTIC WALK 48
   33. THE FAMILY...49
   34. THE GIFT 50
   35. THE FARMER'S HARVEST...51
   36. VIBRANT ARTISTRY..52
   37. THE OLYMPIC SPIRIT...53
   38. THE VOICE 54
   39. THE INHERITANCE...55
   40. THE RESERVOIR...56

DEDICATION

This book is dedicated to my grandmother who I called A-MA in the Taiwanese culture. She recently passed away at the age of 90. Her strong life became my inspiration to write this book. She lived in Taitung, Taiwan and was my only living grandmother alive in 2011. I last saw her in 2010, when my wife and I and our son Joshua visited her during last November. We stayed for eight days but everyday was a blessing to spend time with her. As A-MA (grandmother) has moved on to a better place resting peacefully with God, she will always be listening and her presence will be missed. A-MA, this book is my life's project and a gift to you. I hope you like it.

Your loving grandson

Eddie Ho

ACKNOWLEDGEMENT

The journey of writing this book came from a progression of teachers, dear friends and family members who encouraged me to put my thoughts down on paper. As I wrote, their excitement drew me to write more. I would not be the writer I am today without their help and guidance. At this time, I want to thank the persons who impacted my decision to write my first poetry book. So here it goes.

First, I want to give thanks to my loving wife Amy and my son Joshua who have been the inspiration for writing this book. They have inspired me to always see that family makes the heart grow fonder. I hope that when Joshua grows older, he will enjoy reading his father's words to develop his own ideas through them. When you devote time to your family, you'll develop many stories to share, and these impacted my decision to write this poetry book.

Second, I give thanks to God for the gifts he has bestowed on me. He has blessed me with a wonderful family and the ability to use my mind to enrich others through the power of the pen. It is because of God that I am living a dream to share my poetry with others. I hope that my poems will help people cope with life challenges. I believe God puts people on this earth for a purpose and when you use your gifts, you honor God.

Third, I want to thank my parents for their support of me to obtain a great education. They were always there to support me and through every experience helped me to understand that life always gives people a second chance to shine. I wasn't the best student in the beginning but became a great one at the end who earned an education like no other. I became a teacher with my parent's support. I guess my parents will always think of me as a late bloomer, but like I say, "it's never too late to shine." I love them with all of my heart for what they have taught me.

Fourth, I want to thank Mr. Paul Rallion who helped me critique my book. He was always willing to help me out and to read my text. He provided me with sound advice to make my book stronger. For that, I owe him my deepest thanks. Thanks for helping me. I will always remember your kindness. I am so lucky to have a great friend and colleague to work with.

Fifth, I would like to thank all of my experiences I have had as special education teacher. It taught me how to understand what people face and how students' misbehavior became my inspiration for many of my poems. I wasn't a model student or one who made outstanding grades but I learned how to overcome challenges that I couldn't control. When I understand that, my learning soared to which I became a teacher. As I continue to be a teacher, I will always share the perspective of being a special education student. We all have certain drawbacks that affect our learning style; therefore, we can learn different things from all students. It's not always the brightest ones that teach us the priceless wonders. Remember that.

PART I

The School Days

The Spartan Oath

* Eddie Ho *

I'm rising to achieve
All the things that I have learned
I'm creating historic opportunities
Around every single turn

It's time to look within and stop fooling around
Keep your feet firmly planted to the ground
So wake up STUDENTS, address your purpose in life
Is it to gain knowledge, so stop the gripes?

So give it your all with your pride displayed,
You'll see the results; you'll be amazed
So stop feeling sorry, when we make a mistake
Keep trying to succeed; it's never too late

So lift up your spirit and display your belief
It shapes your true colors of what your classmates will see,
So remember to persevere and give it your all
In a matter of seconds, you'll be walking tall

So reach for the goals you have set in stone
When you attain them, they are yours to own
Never let others put your efforts in despair
Harness your potential to soar throughout the air

Cherish every moment to embrace your feats
Your search for knowledge has made you complete
Continue to aspire by learning something new,

Learning never stops, it's a part of what we do

Learning never stops, it's a part of what we do

Tailspin

• EDDIE HO •

I'm falling so abruptly
About to hit the ground
I have no sense of direction
Nor if I'll be found

I'm descending from the sky
Peeking down to view
I see my life's perspective
Spinning out of hue

I have a big decision
It's not an easy chore
I'm stuck with many notions
I don't know what to explore

I'm here to reaffirm
The choices that I seek
I hope I choose the right ones
In the days that seem so bleak

A Student's Plea

• EDDIE HO •

I'm trying my best to understand
To compute the answer as fast as I can
I'm deliberately not trying to get under your skin
I'm a spirited child, and that's how I've been

So teacher, can you please change your approach
In teaching me to learn by giving me hope
Can you try slowing down the pace so I can succeed?
Don't you ever displace your belief in me!

I've known my efforts weren't really sound
I've made many excuses that made you frown
I've generated the courage to apologize
For that teacher, please sympathize

I've digested some skills that you didn't think I know
I just want to take time to thank you so
I might not have earned the grades you sought
But I will always remember what you taught

I will never give up that easily
When I get intimidated on a task
I will persevere through every activity
To obtain the best education I lack

I will study with relent passion
To earn a worthy degree
I have awoke just in time
To state my valiant decree

The Pulse

* EDDIE HO *

I'm putting my life on the line
To compete with society that moves
Who's looking to earn hefty dollar signs
In the manner of choices I choose

I've been attached to my smart phone
Who loves to sit around and text
I didn't pay any attention in class
To whatever the teacher said next

I relied too much on technology
That my brain is at its wits
I am overloaded with anxiety
Now I'm ready to quit

I didn't see any justice
To work to earn good grades
I was easily distracted
Which caused my grades to fade

I've wasted a free education
Who didn't learn a thing
I'll encounter a life of difficulty
To struggle for every dream

The Identity Crisis

* Eddie Ho *

I'm searching for an identity
To make my reputation known
I'm yearning to be popular
Everywhere I roam

I don't know what to expect
When I walk into every class
Will others like me for who I am
Or will they just simply laugh?

I can't describe that feeling
Why others would strive to be you
Who may not do the right thing
Or be honest to tell the truth

Will I make any friends?
That I don't have to buy
Will I have to lose my identity?
To have them by my side

What will it eventually take?
For my identity to be revealed
Will it lead me to happiness?
To win their everlasting appeal

The Smoking Peers

❖ EDDIE HO ❖

I didn't want to smoke
I just wanted to fit in
I thought it'd make me cool
To be everyone's next of kin

I saw many people smoking
Who were sharing every puff?
The smoke was so overbearing
That I already had enough

I couldn't stand to socialize
When the rooms were full of smoke
I began to have trouble breathing
I felt that I was going to choke

I spent my daily allowance
To buy a single pack
That every time I smoked
The odor clung to my back

I couldn't live another day
Without a cigarette to light
I tried every technique to quit
But regressed with my might

I walked around the cemetery
Thinking I didn't act smart
I shouldn't have let my peers
Influence me from the start

The Test Drive

* EDDIE HO *

I'm driving my mind to death
To keep with this rigorous pace
I don't have time to comprehend
The things that I'm interested in

I'm not getting any sleep
Because the teachers don't let up
The teachers attach more work
Even when you fuss

I'm not resistance to work
But this drive is neither pure
You only care about testing
Not what I'll have to endure

I wish you'd spend the time
To put yourself in my shoes
Will you like to learn that way?
I place the question upon you

I'd rather drive the scenic route
Taking the time to stop
Planning short excursions
To teach what the books forgot

I feel that we are stepped on
That our voices are never heard
Our efforts seem to go unnoticed
It because of these hi-class jerks

The testing is never adequate
That mandates what children learn
It's time to burn that pacing plan
To provide what students yearn

If you are willing to do this
You'll discover what student can do
If you'd invest the time
To accept our point of view

I'm Learning

❖ EDDIE HO ❖

I've relied on myself
To learn everything
Knowing I could
Create my opportunities

I relied on formulas
To help me get by
Which made learning easier
That studying was a fly

I learned to share
My points of view
Speaking with tact
To others too

I began to see
The meanings behind
Which made me think
Of other designs

I learned to work
As hard as I can
To meet the deadlines
That the teacher demands

Realize learning can be fun
Set you mind to get it done
Remember that effort can inspire
To lift our spirits higher and higher

The Delivery

* EDDIE HO *

I once had an assignment
That asked each child to speak
Who had to deliver a speech
For the teacher to critique

I hadn't spoken in public
Nor in front of my peers
Would I make it through?
Via their grueling stares

I thought for a while
To come with a list
The more I thought
My mind got the fits

I finally chose car racing
It was something I've known
Watching various car races
Speeding as they go

I spent some time
To gather the facts
Finding little pieces
To pick up the slack

When it came time
For me to deliver
I became nervous
As my body shivered

When I finished my speech
And returned to my seat
I found a decent grade
That I had achieved

The speech wasn't perfect
It needed to be refined
It could have been better
If I had spent the time

The Regretful Student

* EDDIE HO *

I'm living my life on my own time
Where I get to be the boss
I get to do all sorts of things
When I ditch school and take time off

I'm living to please others
Because they are my only family
I'm living underneath an overpass
Because I have no money

I'm living with dirty clothes
Nor do I have any new ones left
I can't hear the trains go by
Because I'm going deaf

I'm living out here to brave the cold
Struggling to make a dime
I wish that I had stayed in school
To create a new life that shined

The Mark

· Eddie Ho ·

I'm making my mark in society
By remembering my hometown roots
I'm capturing every still portrait
On how my character fits the mood

I've earned the right to be here
Because of the time that I put in
I've worked many dead-end jobs
Making friendships everywhere I've been

I've learned to listen with attentiveness
When I made it to the next plateau
I'm implementing each skill with happiness
Utilizing wisdom to navigate where I'll go

I've found that life can be sweet
When I work hard from the start
Who never refused to give up
The legacy of the mark

PART II

The Unfortunate Incidents

The Defect

* EDDIE HO *

I was born into a family
With an unforeseen birth defect
The doctors tried to diagnose it
But simply could not detect

I could not function properly
To move my limbs around
I felt that I was punished
For being born right now

I stood alone to ponder
The difficulties I would face
I wish that I was never born
So my existence could be erased

I faced the difficult situation
To relearn every skill
Who had to be ambitious
To persist with an iron will

I thought of many ways
To overcome my disadvantage
It taught me to keep on trying
In how I walked or managed

I fought for every opportunity
That I was blatantly denied
Who had to prove to others
That I was perfectly fine

I didn't let that defect
Destroy what I wanted to do
Who kept on working hard
To finish everything I pursued

The Lonely Road

• Eddie Ho •

I'm traveling on a lonely road
With no companion by my side
I'm burdened with a heavy load
Who can't walk another stride

I'm working on a plantation
Struggling to harvest the corn
I'm determined to finish the job
But my shoes are tattered and torn

I'm waiting to receive hot food
A portion from my master
I hope that I can runaway
To live a life thereafter

I probably will not see tomorrow
When they find that I have left
I will emerge with great sorrow
For what I will soon regret

I hope somebody will come
To rescue me by the hand
I hope you'll find my location
To guide me to the Promised Land

I've endured a life of struggles
That impacted my chosen paths
I'll honor how others intervened
In teaching me what I lacked

The Orphan

* Eddie Ho *

I was just a little child
Who was abandoned at the door
I didn't know the reasons
Why my life had been scorned

I grew up pondering the question
Why parents would give me up
Did I cause them any trouble?
To make their lives so tough

I lied awake on a bunk bed
Hoping to hear good news
That a family would adopt me
Who would take a chance on you

Many days passed
Until a couple came by
Who desperately wanted me
Boy, was I surprised

The couple adopted me
Who took me in to love
They accepted me into their family
To make me one of

I knew I didn't look like them
But that really didn't matter
I'm working on a new beginning
That I didn't want to shatter

I had dealt with so many hardships
Mere words couldn't justify
I've become a part of this family
To where I will reside

The Stray Life

* Eddie Ho *

I am running on sheer adrenaline
After running away from home
I haven't got a place to stay
I guess I'd better roam

I wasn't very responsible
When I didn't plan each step
I found myself entering a world
That I desperately wanted to forget

I thought about running wide
To get out from this funk
Whatever remedy I tried
The further more I sunk

I finally got a job
That paid a little wage
It taught me a valuable lesson
That I shouldn't have strayed

I saved a little money
To find a way back there
Would I make there alive?
Or would I end up in despair

I decided to keep on walking
As a car pulled by my side
A man rolled down his window
Asked me if I needed a ride

I asked him where are you going?
The man responded Philly
Could you drop me off?
At the outskirts of the city

The man drove down the route
That led to a familiar road
Next thing I remembered
I had made it home

I woke up the next morning
Having to explain where I've been
I vowed to follow my parents' instructions
Never to defy them once again

The Sticky Situation

◆ EDDIE HO ◆

I have a sticky situation
That is too grand to solve
I have no sense of direction
In how it will get resolved

It has multiplied into a monster
That has created havoc in my life
It has made me scream and holler
That has elevated my levels of strife

I am searching for every angle
To get out of this ridiculous mess
I am seeking guidance to untangle
With any person who I can address

If I don't declare a solution,
The situation will get worse
It will end with a swift execution
That follows me around like a curse

So clear every situation, before you die
It will point out the things to realize
Remember that life is not easy to handle
Without their help, it becomes dismantled

Speculation

* Eddie Ho *

I wandered around my hometown
To speculate what's gone wrong
What had caused the town's meltdown?
That once was booming and strong

I saw so many businesses
That once opened their doors
The windows were boarded shut
That once had been the core

A local gang crept in
To ruin the mighty town
Families moved out quickly
Who no longer stuck around

Many people remained
Then turned to crime
Who ended up in jail?
To pay a hefty price

Nothing lasts forever
Things do change
Life moves forward
By what remains

Juvenile Hall

• Eddie Ho •

I've been in and out of Juvenile Hall
When I was only eight
I was a boy, oh so small
Who didn't know how to relate

I got into some local trouble
When I started boosting car
I tried to outrun the cops
Who didn't get very far

I was sent back to Juvenile Hall
For committing other crimes
Who worked for a local gang
Hoping to hit the big time

I had to visit my Probation Officer
To talk about my recklessness
I had to talk about each incident
To which I didn't want to address

I found a book to read
That detailed a life like mine
It said that if I didn't straighten up
I'd be buried before I turned nine

This message made me think
That my attitude was the disease
I vowed to change something
Or else my life would cease

The Shelter

● Eddie Ho ●

My life is unstable
It is about to crash
I formed a cradle
All I see is the ash

I have no room left here
As the fire grew and grew
I don't know where I sleep tonight
Or if the shelter has any room

I haven't eaten for many days
As I dug throughout the trash
I've slept in smelly cardboard boxes
Because I didn't have any cash

I still yearn for a better life
Despite my recent position
I am just an ordinary person
With a pleasant disposition

So, don't ever discount me
For how I am simply dressed
I hope you will take me seriously
By the talents that I possess

The Blind Eye

• EDDIE HO •

I woke up one Sunday morning
To discover I couldn't see
I didn't know how this occurred
Or why it happened to me

I tried my best to maneuver around
But bumped into everything near
I landed in an awkward position
Who yelled out a scream of fear?

The adjustments came with difficulty
That brought me so much despair
Could I survive to exist in this world?
To show how much I was scared

I had to become a student again
Who relied on my sense of touch?
I taught myself to read in Braille
To detect words with raised bumps

I didn't let this unfortunate incident
Deny what I wanted to pursue
I had to change my disposition
To show others what I could do

The Innocent Victims

* Eddie Ho *

My parents had stopped at a traffic light
When two cars raced down the street
Who collided into my parents' car
That left my father pinned to his seat

My mother laid there wondering
When would the help arrive?
Who prayed with steady devotion?
To keep my father alive

My father was flown to the hospital
Where doctors were standing by
Who all shared one concern?
That time was on their side

My father needed surgery
To stop the bleeding
Who was fighting for his life?
As he laid there pleading

My father look drained
His body looked frail
He had to remain in bed
To recover to get well

My father had to relearn
Many essential things
Like how to use his lungs
To breathe with ease

He'll cherish his life
That has been spared
Who received a miracle?
That God loves never fails

PART III

Occupational Status

The Company

* EDDIE HO *

I've joined a company of brothers
Who understood their roles and deeds
They're dedicated to helping others
Who fight the battle overseas

These folks we call them soldiers
Who protect our freedom and rights
It's because of their ultimate service
Our babies can sleep well at night

I've heard these brothers are notorious
For always doing what is right
These brothers guard our nation
By protecting the borders at night

They will never abort a mission
When a brother has been shot
They will drag him to safety
With all the might they got

These families tremble with fear
When they watch the nightly news
Hoping it's not their turn
To hear their son is gone

The company keeps on going
To honor their fallen brothers
Whose actions will be preserved
For what they gave to others

Dr. Grinny Ho

◦ EDDIE HO ◦

I served as a doctor
In a town I used to know
I delivered over 6000 babies
That was called Sikeston, MO

I received my medical school training
From a college in Taiwan
Who sponsored Asian doctors
That's why I did respond

I quickly got accustomed
From moving my family there
I learned how things functioned
In a town of Southern flair

I built up my medical practice
By treating patients who couldn't pay
I accepted what they could give me
Any gifts that came my way

I didn't become a doctor
For the money and prestige
I honored that Hippocratic Oath
To help those desperately in need

I provided them with feedback
In diagnosing what was wrong
I performed many operations
That sometimes lasted so long

I realized that being a doctor
Patients have a right to choose
Whether to follow my advice
Or you'll continue feeling blue

I practiced for over 22 years
When I retired at 47 years of age
Who met so many wonderful people
That reflected why I stayed

The Pastor

* EDDIE HO *

I was reading the Bible
When I heard the voice
Who revealed I'd be a pastor
Throughout my whole life

I opened up my heart to follow
What God had sacrificed?
Who gave his only son Jesus
To bring me eternal life

I went to Fuller Seminary
To interpret the scriptures
Where I digested its meanings
As my faith in him got richer

I served in many capacities
Before I got ordained
Who lent out my ears
To hear what people faced

I remembered that day
When I gave my first sermon
Who became so energetic
As the verses kept flowing

I led my congregation
To show how God is true
Who gives us every blessing?
When the time is due

I went on mission trips
To lead the church abroad
When ventured to remote areas?
To teach aboriginals about God

God's work is so uplifting
There's always so much to do
When you give your life to him
He'll always be there for you

The Teacher

❋ EDDIE HO ❋

There is a teacher in all of us
That inspires each child to dream
Exhausting every single measure
To ensure every child succeed

The teacher stimulates the child's mind
How the past influences the modern day
Who bridges the ideas of old and new
To watch what children might say

The teacher provides the children with tools
Who transforms each piece into a skill
The teacher guides how they alter their mind
To bring themselves joy and thrills

The teacher watches from a distance
To applaud what the child has done
Hoping to infuse the passion
That learning can be fun

The teacher will have a dynamic power
To cherish every moment they serve
Who will face many uphill challenges
To win the respect that they deserve

The Social Worker

* Eddie Ho *

I visited so many chaotic homes
Where life was such a disaster
I entered a converted garage
That raised my emotions thereafter

I saw so many filthy kitchens
With nothing left to spare
The rooms were hot and musty
That there was not even any fresh air

How could anyone live in this condition?
To care for an infant child or two
How could anyone neglect their obligations?
To give their children shelter, clothes and food

I acted by removing the children
Until that family got a firm grip
On what was their ultimate duty
That's gotten them in dire shit

What's the world coming to?
That my work comes with despair
Where families are torn with issues
Who struggle with their own welfare

No child should ever live like that
It's time to show our concern
To help these innocent children
Live a life without ridicule or scorn

The Entertainer

* EDDIE HO *

It is all about the music
That I am dying to play
Spun with a rocking melody
That makes people hum it all day

Who cares how people interpret it
For the words are what they are
I will play my set to everyone
That comes from nations afar

I am sharing my music
To the role of ambassador
Which will heal a world in crisis
That unites everyone thereafter

I owe every little performance
For the ability to entertain
I blessed with this wonderful journey
By the memories of lives I changed

The Question Mark

* Eddie Ho *

What have I done?
To earn this role
Where society judges a character
By the knowledge I know?

Can I fool anyone?
Who is depending on me
To share my inner thoughts
On what is reality?

Will anyone trust me?
To pilot their ship
Will I be taken seriously
When I firmly take the grip?

So plan each step
To take control
Rev up the jet engines
To let learning flow

Question everything
When the time has come
To dedicate this role
On a job well done

The Coach

◆ EDDIE HO ◆

I've always been a coach
Who took players under my wings?
That recruited many prolific players
Who came here to live their dreams?

I held many practices
That lasted for hours
Where players kept working
To build up their power

I positioned every player
To exercise their talents
Who walked on the field?
To display their magic

I taught them how to handle
A win or a defeat
Who were always winners?
Each time we compete

I inspired my players
To work hard in class
Earning every honor
To eventually pass

I've given my life
To be their coach
Who's lasted this long
By my approach

The Status Symbol

* Eddie Ho *

What is the value of status?
That people consider as wealth
Is it driving a luxurious car?
That makes them look so stealth

Why am I doing this?
To bluff that I am rich
Or am I doing this
To fit into a particular niche

Can I really afford this car?
With the payments so high
Will I be accepted on credit?
Or will I be simply denied

How will I ever get this car?
That I promised my boss I had
Will I still have that high-paying job?
That I fought so hard to get

What will you end up with?
As money goes down the drain
Will it amount to a victory?
Or will it lead to shame

I'm hoping that I will not
Have to reveal my true status
Who spends their life buying?
Every material apparatus

PART IV

The Priceless Wonders

A New Life

* EDDIE HO *

I see a distant image
Guiding me to a foreign land
I don't know what its purpose
On what I'm supposed to understand

I am traveling throughout the atmosphere
On a vehicle with unlimited gears
Whose propelled me to realize
That I must overcome my fears

I mustn't neglect the gifts
That encompasses who I am
I am learning from experience
To construct beauty with my hands

I'm using my human body
To shield me from the cold weather
I'm embracing the world of biology
To make the lives of everyone better

I've placed my trust in its observation
For what I needed to change
I will reach every destination
With the goodness that remains

I'll dedicate a word of prayer
To share my utmost gratitude
It gave me a sense of direction
To bring my life some latitude

The Romantic Walk

* EDDIE HO *

I remember the day
When we first met
A rose caught my eye
That I will never forget

I got the nerve to ask your name
From then on, my life had changed
I listened so attentively when you spoke
The love I felt had just awoke

I remembered each time
We chatted on the line
I expressed who I was
To hope you'd be mine

I brought over flowers
To ask you out
You smiled to let me know
That there was no doubt

It didn't take us long
To travel abroad
Capturing every moment
With vivid snapshots

It brought two parties
From different lands
Whose love for one another
Has continued to stand

The Family

* EDDIE HO *

The family is the cornerstone
That makes a house walls stand
The family is that special unit
That will never really disband

The family honors their promise
By teaching others as they go
The family supports each member
By devoting the time to do so

The family never lets the conflicts
Destroy the value that they have built
The family talks out their differences
Before they speak hastily with silt

The family learns to adore one another
In the times they may not agree
The family learns to forgive wrongdoing
By teaching every member to see

The family builds up the memories
Snapping the portraits from every view
The family laughs with jubilation
By sharing what each member can do

The family is the sacred institution
Where its luster had lost its shine
The family is that one unique place
Where mind and lives can be intertwined

The Gift

∗ EDDIE HO ∗

The children are the ultimate heroes
Who make our lives so complete
The children showcase their wisdom
By expressing truly what they see

The children bring us laughter
By making every moment count
The children explore new dimensions
By illustrating what they are about

The children walk with bravery
As they gradually take some risks
The children learn about responsibility
In making the right choices that fits

The children touch our lives
In many ways we will never know
The children are God's Blessings
That make our families whole

The children are the ones
Who inspire us to get out of bed?
The children will be the ones
Who will lead us when we're dead

The Farmer's Harvest

* Eddie Ho *

I have savored the farmer's harvest
That brings goodness from the ground
Which restores my weary stamina
That has turned my energy around

I smelled a fragrant aroma
Of a meal being prepared
It made me tingle with envy
Wondering how will it compare

I ate the dish slowly
Treasuring every bite
Who had to get that recipe?
That's cured my appetite

I delivered the farmer's harvest
To feed every hungry nation
So children will live on
By my heart of dedication

Vibrant Artistry

❖ EDDIE HO ❖

I live in a magnificent world
Where colors are everywhere
They complement the canvas
Displayed for people to compare

These colors bring out the person
Who uses a brush to create a form?
It could be concrete or abstract
But may not always be uniform

This canvas reveals its vibrancy
As the colors are assembled into view
Which resembles a majestic painting?
By it unique array of hue

It will attract a flock of people
To admire its splendid view
Who value its elements of artistry?
To interpret its endless virtue

The Olympic Spirit

* Eddie Ho *

The games are beginning
There is nothing to fear
The teams have arrived
To show why they're here

The competition is set into overdrive
Make your prediction which athlete will shine?
So give it your all as you compete without duress
To stand upon the podium with the fastest time set

It doesn't matter whether you medaled in the heat
Just give it your best shot as you compete
So remember the promise that you vowed
When you return home, you'll feel so proud

So honor that spirit through every quest
To become the world's very best
When the day comes to say goodbye
I'll remember this memory for a lifetime

The Voice

* Eddie Ho *

I'm thinking about a heavenly voice
Who listens to my prayers?
That's provided me with necessities
When my life was in despair

I couldn't escape from this voice
As I tried to find common ground
Who sounded his mighty thunder?
To keep people pure and sound

The voice was there to accompany me
Wherever I chose to roam
It has protected me everyday
To make it safely home

I kept on trusting this voice
As it laid out my life's plan
Who opened many doors?
To create the person I am

I listened with obedience
Even when things went wrong
I interpreted every scripture
To keep my spirit strong

Where will this voice take me?
It's not for me to say
I'll abide by his teaching
To share my faith everyday

The Inheritance

* Eddie Ho *

I will inherit the kingdom
When I first chose
To follow your lead
Everywhere I go

I will devote my life to the text
Keeping the faith to whatever comes next
I will live my life in servitude
Sharing your message with others too

I will teach others how to give and receive
To help those people who are desperately in need
So believe it or not, despite what people do?
The Lord will forgive and love us too

I will follow every commandment
That brings harmony to my life
I will use every gift bestowed
To honor you with my might

When problems arise, don't focus on despair
Always keep praying that God is forever there
So jump on board to cherish this flight
To inherit God's kingdom that's out of sight

The Reservoir

❖ Eddie Ho ❖

I'm standing here at the reservoir
Wondering did I neglect anything?
Who's searching for the meaning of life
With the collected objects I bring

I bring forth to the reservoir
A paper with a name and date
It symbolizes my beginning
Which the Lord hath create

I hold up some type of transcript
That states I've earned a degree
Who graduated from a college
Unaware of where I will be

I found a torn piece of paper
That displayed an amount
Did I work for these companies?
Who spent hours handling their accounts

I must have been married
To someone I've known
I've glanced at this certificate
That's made my family whole

I discovered a document
That looked like a deed
Who stated I was the owner
To raise a family of three

I bought this house
For my wife and son
Who delighted my life
For years to come

As I grow older, there's no time to waste
Spend it with your family before it too late
Whatever happens in life, enjoy every view
Did my life really matter to you?

ABOUT THE AUTHOR

The inspiration for The Edge came when his church youth group went on a mission trip to Paducah, Kentucky to work in the soup kitchens. While working there, author Eddie Ho met ordinary people who had suffered a mere setback in their life and were homeless and hungry. They had no control over what had happened, nor did they think their lives were over. Through getting to know some of them, they taught him that life is about how we inspire one another to overcome a difficult struggle not to judge how they got there. Since that time, he has never forgotten those words to let the power of his pen do the talking for him. The words that flow from his pen serve to provide an uplifting message that the greatest lessons are in which we come to aid a person in need, than constantly thinking about ourselves. He continues to serve as a special education teacher in Los Angeles.